COCKTAILS

GW00705947

COCKTAILS

Joyce Nutley, FHCIMA

Head of Food and Beverage Service Section,
Thames Valley College, Slough

Headway · Hodder & Stoughton

British Library Cataloguing in Publication Data

ISBN 0 340 52681 5

First published 1990

© 1990 Joyce Nutley

Typeset by Litho Link Ltd, Welshpool, Powys, Wales.
Printed in Hong Kong for Hodder and Stoughton
Educational, a division of Hodder and Stoughton Ltd,
Mill Road, Dunton Green, Sevenoaks, Kent by
Colorcraft Ltd, Hong Kong

CONTENTS

INTRODUCTION

This book has been designed as a functional, indispensable manual for all cocktail makers/shakers. It provides:

- a wide variety of alcoholic and non-alcoholic cocktails to suit all ages, tastes and occasions
- an alphabetical list for quick reference
- a cocktail a page
- clear, concise instructions
- a colour photograph per cocktail for perfect presentation
- colour coding according to the main ingredient for easy cocktail selection suggestion
- an essential 'aide-mémoire' for professional bartenders and hosts/hostesses alike

Cocktails is a vital ingredient for all successful cocktail makers. Home entertainers will find it invaluable in selecting, preparing and presenting cocktails for those special events. It will also be useful for hotel and catering managers, trainees, students, bar staff, steward and stewardesses throughout the entire industry. In particular *Cocktails* will be invaluable to all students studying on City & Guilds 700/8, 707/1/2/4, 717 and 720 courses, for the BTEC First Certificates and Diplomas, National Diploma, HNC and Higher National Diploma, for examinations leading to membership of the HCIMA and for Limited Skill Certificates, Caterbase programmes and Degree level courses.

Why not start at 'A' and finish with 'Z'.

Good shaking!!

In a Parisian bar

A BRIEF HISTORY

Cocktails are the designer drink of today, with a wide choice to suit every age, taste and occasion. The origin of the word 'cocktail' is unclear, but there are numerous suggestions:

Coquetel a mixed drink from the Bordeaux region of France, served to French officers serving in the USA
Cock-ale a mixture of spirits given to fighting cocks in the eighteenth century in England and used as a toast to the victorious bird
Cock-tailed the docking of horse's tail to indicate a horse of mixed stock – a cocktail – not a thoroughbred
Coquetiers a type of egg cup used by a French physician to serve his mixed drinks to American friends
Vive le cocktail Betsy Flanagan an Irish tavern keeper in USA served mixed drinks from bottles decorated with cocks feathers; a Frenchman in proposing a toast declared "Vive le cocktail!"

Without a doubt, whatever the origin, everyone agrees the Cocktail Age started in earnest in the Prohibition Era in USA 1920–1933. It was an ingenious idea to mix several drinks together and so disguise the doubtful origins, aromas and purity of illicit liquor. Prohibition was repealed in 1933 and liquor standards raised so cocktail creations and contents became more refined. Cocktails became respectable and have continued to improve and develop to become the drinking vogue for all.

At the new Café Royal

Cocktails range from elegant 'classics' (like Dry Martini, Manhattan and Sidecar) to the fun, colourful, exotic creations (like Harvey Wallbanger, Pinacolada, and Tequila Sunrise). Cocktails are drinks with glamour, style and charisma.

THE MEASURE

All measures listed use the professional bar measure called a 'Jigger', which can be purchased combining the 6 out (⅚ fluid ounce) and the 3 out (1⅔ fluid ounce) measure – a worthwhile investment for the cocktail maker. Alternatively, the 6 out measure can be replaced by a liqueur glass and the 3 out measure by a sherry glass.

All cocktails listed are for one serving.

Measures quoted may be increased or decreased but *ratios* of ingredients should remain constant.

GLASSWARE

Glassware for cocktails varies in shape, size and character. A well mixed drink will taste good no matter in what glass it is served, but custom dictates that certain drinks are more appropriately served in certain shaped glasses. Generally this is due to the quantity and mixture of the drink.

It is important that all glassware is scrupulously clean and sparkling. To check for cleanliness, the selected glass should be held up to the light and repolished with a dry, fine linen cloth if necessary. It should then be held up to the light and rechecked.

Cocktails taste better when served ice cold. It is wise to chill the glass by filling it with ice cubes and soda water whilst preparing the cocktail. The glass is then emptied just prior to pouring the cocktail.

In this book the most suitable glass has been selected for each cocktail. The glassware used is listed below.

Brandy balloon
Short stemmed balloon bowl glass, wide at base and narrow at rim. The shape allows for the full aroma of the drink to be trapped and appreciated.

Champagne saucer
A stemmed glass with a wide saucer-shaped bowl; its shape allows excess bubbles from sparkling wines to escape. Sometimes referred to as a 'champagne coupe'.

Cocktail glass

Designed with the cocktail drinker in mind, it has a long slim stem for ease of holding. The warmth of the hand does not therefore warm the cocktail and detract from the quality and taste. The curved shaped bowl creates style and character.

Collins (10 fluid ounce)

Tall, straight-sided tumbler for those extra-long cocktails, eg Zombies, Collins.

Highball (8 fluid ounce)

Tall straight-sided tumbler used for long cocktails, eg Cuba Libre, Punches, Noggs, Pimms.

Lowball (5 fluid ounce)

Short tumbler with sloping sides. Used for Bloody Mary and other similar drinks.

Martini glass

Stemmed glass with 'V' shaped bowl. An elegant glass for classics such as Martinis and Daiquiri.

Old Fashioned (8 fluid ounce)

Tumbler with sloping sides. Used for Mists, Gibson, Americano etc.

Paris goblet

Short stemmed, round bowled standard wine glass. Ideal for Black Velvet, Prairie Oyster.

Sour glass (5 fluid ounce)

Stemmed glass with tall, slim bowl that curves in slightly at rim. This allows sparkling drinks to retain effervescence for longer.

EQUIPMENT

Cocktail shaker

Made of stainless steel or silver in three sections:

    (a) the base for ingredients

    (b) a top with built-in strainer which fits tightly over the base

    (c) a cap which covers the top allowing the cocktail to be shaken

    The strained cocktail is poured from the shaker into the appropriate glass.

    Note: cocktails are stirred when all the ingredients are clear.

Mixing glass

Used for stirred cocktails. A glass jug without a handle, but with a lip for easy pouring. Requires use of a hawthorn strainer to strain the cocktail into the correct glass.

Hawthorn strainer
Stainless steel or silver flat short-handled strainer with spring coiled on exterior. This allows for tight fitting in the top of the mixing glass or glass section of a Boston shaker.

Barspoon
Spiralled, long-handled teaspoon with flat muddler end. The muddler is used for crushing sugar and mint as necessary.

Blender
Used especially for drinks containing puréed fruits or for preparing large quantities of a particular cocktail.

Measures
A 'Jigger' or measure is a means of measuring and controlling the quantity of liquid ingredients. A Jigger, combining the 6 out (⅚ fluid ounce) and the 3 out (1⅔ fluid ounce) measures, is a must to ensure the consistency of the selected cocktail.

ADDITIONAL USEFUL EQUIPMENT

The following useful equipment should be readily available in a truly professional cocktail bar:

Waiter's friend/corkscrew: for opening bottles
Bottle stopper: for sealing opened bottles of sparkling wine
Ice buckets: for storage of ice cubes (plentiful supply essential)
Ice tongs: for hygienic dispensing of ice
Ice crusher: for easy preparation from ice cubes
Chopping board/working surfaces: for garnish preparation
Bar knife: for preparing garnishes; tonged end for 'picking up' garnish
Canelle knife: for removing zest for garnish
Teaspoon: for ingredient measuring
Juice extractor: for fresh fruit juice preparation

Crown cork opener: for removing bottle tops
Wine cooler: for champagne chilling
Fine linen cloths: for glassware polishing
Bar mats: to absorb moisture/spillage from bar top

Paper goods
Paper goods are used to enhance the presentation of the cocktail:

Swizzle stick: for stirring drinks
Coasters: for underneath the cocktail glass
Cocktail napkins: for drinker's convenience
Cocktail sticks: for presenting cocktail garnishes
Straws: of assorted colours, lengths, sizes and shapes
Doyleys: for perfect presentation when using underplates for cocktail service
Parasols: for exotic, fun, colourful presentation

INGREDIENTS

The majority of the cocktails in this book are based on the following main ingredients: gin, vodka, rum whisky, wine, vermouth, and other various spirits and minerals (in the case of non-alcoholic drinks).

Additional extras
Miscellaneous ingredients should be plentiful and to hand to enable an efficient cocktail service to be offered. These additional extras can be displayed on silver salvers on bar tops to help promote cocktail sales.

The most frequently used ingredients include: olives, cocktail onions, salt and pepper, nutmeg (grated), tabasco sauce, cayenne pepper, Worcester sauce, tomato ketchup, Angostura bitters, sugar syrup (gomme), grenadine syrup, almond syrup (orgeat), rosewater, castor sugar, sugar cubes, coffee beans, eggs, milk, cream, yoghurt, raisins, honey, tea, coconut cream.

GARNISHES

Garnishes should be stored correctly to maintain perfect condition. They should be prepared only to order to retain their crispness, freshness and juiciness.

A garnish should be appropriate for the selected cocktail, according to the ingredients, and should be used to create a good, balanced, visual impression. It should not be used to overdress a cocktail or cause embarrassment or inconvenience to the drinker. Garnishes should enhance a cocktail and create an exotic drink experience.

Garnishes used include: cocktail cherries, lemons, limes, oranges, pineapple, coconut, apples, mint, kiwi fruit, strawberries, mint and cucumber.

A garnish is the final colourful touch which completes the selected cocktail. Cocktails can be dressed up with:

Fruit which is cut into different shapes and thicknesses: slices, triangles, semi-circles, slithers, zest spirals, twists

Mint leaves: which should be lightly crushed to impart flavour (as should citrus peel)

Cucumber skin: which is best peeled to extract the delicate flavour

Cocktail cherries: which are available in various colours, the natural red being the most versatile

Garnish preparation allows for individual creativity and ingenuity.

MAKING COCKTAILS

'Frosting' glassware
Dip the rim of glass in egg white or lemon juice. Redip in castor sugar or salt. Tidy up 'frosting' if required.

It is usual to 'frost' with sugar those cocktails containing a neutral spirit, ie gin, vodka, white rum. 'Salt frosting' does not appeal to all drinkers.

Checklist

1. Prepare all necessary glassware, ingredients and garnishes. Chill glassware if required
2. Half fill shaker or bar glass with ice and add ingredients
3. Shake or stir vigorously. Never shake any effervescent ingredient
4. Strain carefully into prepared glassware
5. Add garnishes and serve

Taken from Punch, *1922*

SHAKE, STIR OR POUR?

A cocktail is a skilfully blended drink prepared by shaking, stirring or pouring to create an exotic drink experience. It is the ingredients that determine the method:

Shake
(Using a cocktail shaker)
Fruit juice, egg white, egg yolk, cream, milk, or any cloudy ingredient

Stir
(Using a bar glass)
All clear ingredients

Pour
(Using specified presentation glass)
Ingredients of different specific gravities when separate distinct layers are required

Two ladies, one glass

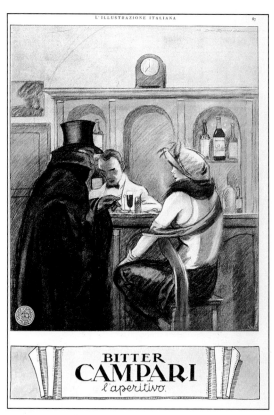

1924 Campari advertisement

RECIPES

$\mathcal{A}$DELAIDE

INGREDIENTS

1 × 6 out gin, 1 × 6 out sweet vermouth,
1 × 6 out lime juice (fresh if possible),
3 dashes grenadine,
1 tablespoon crushed ice,
1 slice lime or lemon

PREPARATION

Place crushed ice in bar glass

Pour gin, vermouth and lime juice over ice

Add grenadine

Stir and strain

Serve in chilled cocktail glass

Garnish with slice of fresh lime or lemon

𝒜LEXANDER

INGREDIENTS

1 × ⅙ out brandy,
1 × ⅙ out crème de cacao,
1 × ⅙ out cream, crushed ice,
grated nutmeg

PREPARATION

¼ fill shaker with crushed ice
Add all ingredients
Shake well
Strain into small cocktail glass
Sprinkle with grated nutmeg

AMERICANO

INGREDIENTS

1 × 6 out Campari,
1 × 3 out sweet vermouth,
soda, 1 orange slice or lemon twist,
6 ice cubes

PREPARATION

Place ice cubes in highball glass

Add Campari and vermouth

Stir well

Top with soda and stir

Garnish with orange slice or lemon twist

Name derived from American style Americano

AMERICAN GLORY

INGREDIENTS

juice of ½ orange,
4 fluid ounces champagne,
1 fluid ounce soda,
1 orange slice, 2 ice cubes

PREPARATION

Place ice cubes in highball glass
Add orange juice and champagne
Top with soda
Garnish with orange slice

APPLEKNOCKER

INGREDIENTS

2 × 6 out Galliano, 1 × 6 out lemon juice,
8 fluid ounces apple juice,
1 lemon slice, 1 apple slice,
5 ice cubes (for shaker),
2 ice cubes (for glass)

PREPARATION

Place ice cubes in shaker
Add Galliano and lemon juice
Shake well and strain into highball glass
Add ice cubes
Top up with apple juice
Garnish with lemon juice and apple slices

Au Revoir

INGREDIENTS

1 × 6 out brandy,
1 × 6 out sloe gin, juice of 1 lemon,
1 egg white, 1 lemon slice,
4 ice cubes

PREPARATION

Place ice cubes in shaker

Add brandy, sloe gin, lemon juice and egg white

Shake well and strain

Pour into cocktail glass

Garnish with lemon slice

*B*ACARDI

INGREDIENTS

1½ × 6 out Cuban rum, juice of 1 lime,
2 dashes grenadine, 1 cocktail cherry,
lemon slice, 1 cocktail stick, 4 ice cubes

PREPARATION

Place ice cubes in shaker

Add lime juice, grenadine and Cuban rum

Shake well and strain

Pour into cocktail glass

Garnish with lemon and cherry on stick

*Very similar to Daiquiri but gets its name
from* RON BACARDI *– the spirit used.*

BENEDICT

INGREDIENTS

1½ × 6 out whisky,
½ × 6 out Benedictine,
½ bottle ginger ale,
lime slice, 2 ice cubes

PREPARATION

Place ice cubes in bar glass
Add whisky and Benedictine and stir well
Pour all into old fashioned glass
Top up with ginger ale
Garnish with lime slice

*B*ETWEEN THE *S*HEETS

INGREDIENTS

½ × 6 out white rum, ½ × 6 out brandy,
½ × 6 out Cointreau,
1 teaspoon lemon juice,
lemon twist, ice cubes

PREPARATION

Place ice cubes in shaker
Add all ingredients
Shake well and strain
Serve in chilled Martini glass
Garnish with lemon twist

*B*LACK *R*USSIAN

INGREDIENTS

1 × 6 out vodka,
½ × 6 out Kahlúa,
ice cubes

PREPARATION

Place ice cubes into lowball glass
Add ingredients
Stir well

B̶lack V̶elvet

INGREDIENTS

½ glass champagne,
½ glass Guinness (stout)

PREPARATION

Fill a Paris goblet or Irish coffee glass with
equal quantities of stout and champagne
Should be drunk as soon as possible

ℬLOODY 𝓜ARY

INGREDIENTS

1 × 3 out vodka, 4 fluid ounces tomato juice,
2 dashes Worcester sauce, 1 dash Tabasco sauce,
2 dashes Angostura bitters, juice of ½ lemon,
pinch of salt and pepper, celery stick,
lemon slice, 1 straw, 5 ice cubes

PREPARATION

Place ice cubes in shaker
Add remaining ingredients excluding garnish
Shake well and strain into a highball glass
Garnish with celery, lemon slice and straw

*Invented by Fernard Petiot working in
Harry's New York Bar, Paris in 1920s and named after
Mary Pickford, actress of the Thirties*

BLUE ARROW

1 × 6 out gin,
½ × 6 out Cointreau,
½ × 6 out lime juice,
½ × 6 out blue Curaçao,
crushed ice

Fill shaker ¾ full with crushed ice

Add gin, Cointreau, lime juice and Curaçao

Shake well and strain

Serve in chilled cocktail glass

𝐵OSOM 𝐶ARESSER

INGREDIENTS

2 × 6 out brandy,
1 × 6 out orange Curaçao,
4 dashes grenadine,
1 egg yolk, 2 fresh cherries,
5 ice cubes

PREPARATION

Place ice cubes in shaker

Add brandy, orange Curaçao, grenadine and egg yolk

Shake well and strain

Serve in chilled champagne saucer

Garnish with cherries

*B*RAINSTORM

INGREDIENTS

1 × 6 out whisky,
1 × 6 out dry vermouth,
1 × 6 out Benedictine,
1 orange slice,
2 tablespoons crushed ice

PREPARATION

Place crushed ice in bar glass
Add whisky, dry vermouth and Benedictine
Stir well and strain
Pour into chilled tulip glass
Garnish with orange slice

BRONX

INGREDIENTS

1 × 6 out gin,
½ × 6 out sweet vermouth,
½ × 6 out dry vermouth,
½ × 6 out orange juice,
2 tablespoons crushed ice,
1 cocktail cherry, 1 cocktail stick

PREPARATION

Place crushed ice in shaker
Add gin, sweet and dry vermouths and orange juice
Shake well and strain
Serve in chilled Martini glass
Garnish with cherry on stick

BUCKS FIZZ

INGREDIENTS

²/₃ glass champagne,
¹/₃ glass orange juice,
1 orange slice,
1 cocktail cherry,
1 cocktail stick

PREPARATION

Place orange juice in chilled champagne saucer
Top up with chilled champagne
Garnish with orange slice and cherry on stick
Serve immediately

*The Englishman's version of Champagne à l'Orange
as served by Bucks Club in London*

CAVENDISH

INGREDIENTS

2 × 6 out vodka,
4 fluid ounces champagne,
2 dashes Angostura bitters,
1 lemon slice,
crushed ice

PREPARATION

Fill a highball glass with crushed ice
Add Angostura bitters and vodka
Top up with champagne
Garnish with lemon slice
Serve immediately

*C*hampagne *C*ocktail

INGREDIENTS

4 fluid ounces champagne,
1 teaspoon brandy, 1 sugar cube,
2 dashes Angostura bitters, 1 orange slice,
1 cocktail cherry, 1 cocktail stick

PREPARATION

Place sugar cube into champagne saucer

Splash Angostura bitters onto cube

Add champagne

Float brandy on top

Garnish with orange slice and cherry on stick

CLOVER CLUB

INGREDIENTS

1 × 6 out gin,
6 dashes grenadine,
1 × 6 out lemon juice,
1 egg white,
crushed ice

PREPARATION

Fill shaker ¾ full with crushed ice
Add gin, grenadine, lemon juice and egg white
Shake well
Strain into chilled cocktail glass

𝒞OFFEE

INGREDIENTS

1½ × 6 out brandy,
½ × 6 out port,
1 teaspoon sugar,
1 egg yolk,
4 ice cubes,
coffee beans

PREPARATION

Place ice cubes in shaker
Add brandy, port, sugar and egg yolk
Shake well
Strain into lowball glass
Garnish with coffee beans

*C*UBA *L*IBRE

INGREDIENTS

1½ × 6 out rum (dark),
1 × 6 out lemon juice,
8 fluid ounces Coca-Cola,
1 lemon slice, 4 ice cubes, 2 straws

PREPARATION

Place ice cubes in highball glass
Add rum, Coca-Cola and lemon juice
Stir
Add lemon slice
Serve with straws

*Popularised during Prohibition by Americans who
could afford to hop over from Florida to Havana*

CUBAN COCKTAIL

INGREDIENTS

1 × 6 out brandy,
½ × 6 out apricot brandy,
juice of ½ lemon,
5 ice cubes,
1 slice kiwi fruit

PREPARATION

Place ice cubes in shaker
Add lemon juice, brandy and apricot brandy
Shake well and strain
Pour into chilled cocktail glass
Garnish with kiwi fruit

*D*AIQUIRI

INGREDIENTS

1 × 3 out rum (white),
4 dashes gomme (sugar syrup),
juice of 2 limes, crushed ice,
1 cocktail cherry, 1 lime slice, 1 cocktail stick

PREPARATION

Fill shaker ¾ full with crushed ice

Add rum, sugar syrup and lime juice

Shake well. Strain into Martini glass

Garnish with cherry on stick and lime

*Named after the Daiquiri Nickel Mine, Cuba
where it was invented for American engineers
during a shortage of imported liquor*

*D*UBONNET *C*OCKTAIL

INGREDIENTS

1 × 6 out gin,
1 × 6 out Dubonnet,
1 lemon rind,
6 ice cubes

PREPARATION

Place ice cubes in bar glass
Add Dubonnet and gin
Stir well
Strain into cocktail glass
Add twist of lemon rind

𝓔DINBURGH

INGREDIENTS

1½ × 6 out whisky,
¼ × 6 out apricot brandy,
¼ × 6 out crème de menthe,
½ × 6 out dry vermouth,
2 dashes Angostura bitters,
5 ice cubes, mint

PREPARATION

Place 4 ice cubes in bar glass

Shake in Angostura bitters

Add whisky, apricot brandy, crème de menthe,
and dry vermouth

Stir very well. Strain into lowball glass

Garnish with mint and ice cube

EGG NOGG

INGREDIENTS

1 whole egg,
1 × 3 out sherry (or any desired spirit),
½ teaspoon powdered sugar,
¼ pint milk,
strawberry, nutmeg

PREPARATION

Into shaker place egg, sherry, powdered sugar and milk
Shake well
Strain into old fashioned glass
Garnish with strawberry
Grate a little nutmeg on top

FERNET BRANCA

INGREDIENTS

1 × 6 out Fernet Branca,
1 dash Pernod,
2 fluid ounces iced water,
2 cherries, 3 ice cubes

PREPARATION

Place ice cubes in old fashioned glass
Pour on Fernet Branca, Pernod and iced water
Garnish with cherries
Drink in one go!

Ideal for hangover – medicinal flavour and aroma

FORESTER

INGREDIENTS

1½ × 6 out vodka, ½ × 6 out sweet vermouth,
½ × 6 out dry vermouth, ½ teaspoon grenadine,
juice of ½ grapefruit, 4 ice cubes,
1 lemon slice, 1 cocktail cherry,
1 cocktail stick, straws

PREPARATION

Place ice cubes in shaker

Add grapefruit juice, grenadine, vodka
and sweet and dry vermouths

Shake well and strain

Pour into chilled old fashioned glass

Garnish with lemon and cherry on stick

Serve with straws

FRUIT CUP

INGREDIENTS

2 × 3 out orange juice,
2 × 3 out grapefruit juice,
2 × 3 out pineapple juice,
2 × 3 out apple juice,
1 slice of apple, 1 slice of lemon,
1 slice of orange, 1 kiwi fruit,
1 strawberry, straws

PREPARATION

Fill shaker ¾ full with ice cubes

Add all fruit juice. Shake well. Pour into highball glass

Decorate with apple, lemon, kiwi and orange slices
and strawberry

Serve with straws

GALLIANO SOUR

INGREDIENTS

1 × 6 out whisky,
1 × 6 out Galliano,
1 × 6 out orange juice,
½ × 6 out lemon juice,
5 – 6 ice cubes,
1 orange wheel

PREPARATION

Place ice cubes in shaker

Add whisky, Galliano, lemon and orange juice

Shake well and strain

Pour into frosted sour or cocktail glass
(frost with sugar)

Garnish with orange wheel

G IBSON

INGREDIENTS

1½ × 6 out gin,
½ × 6 out extra dry sherry,
1 cocktail onion, 1 cocktail stick, 5 ice cubes

PREPARATION

Place ice cubes in bar glass

Pour on sherry and gin

Stir well

Strain into chilled old fashioned glass

Garnish with cocktail onion on stick

*Invented for the artist Charles Dana Gibson
by Charley Connelly, bartender at the
Player's Club, New York during prohibition*

$\mathcal{G}$IMLET

INGREDIENTS

1 × 3 out gin,
1 × 6 out bottled lime juice,
2 tablespoons crushed ice,
1 lime wheel,
straws

PREPARATION

Place crushed ice in shaker

Add lime juice and gin

Shake well and strain

Serve in chilled cocktail glass

Garnish with lime wheel and straws

GIN SLING

INGREDIENTS

1½ × 6 out gin, ½ × 6 out cherry brandy,
½ × 6 out lemon juice, soda, 1 lemon slice,
1 cocktail cherry, 1 cocktail stick, straws,
6 ice cubes

PREPARATION

Place ice cubes in shaker

Add lemon juice, cherry brandy and gin

Shake well and strain. Pour into highball glass

Top up with soda

Garnish with lemon and cherry on stick and straws

*The only survivor of the category of cocktails
known as 'Slings' – could be made with any spirit.
Similar to a Collins*

GIN SOUR

INGREDIENTS

1½ × 6 out gin,
½ × 6 out lemon juice,
3 dashes gomme (sugar syrup),
1 cocktail cherry,
1 cocktail stick,
1 lemon slice, 6 ice cubes

PREPARATION

Place ice cubes in shaker

Pour on lemon juice, sugar syrup and gin

Shake well and strain

Serve in sour glass

Garnish with cherry on stick and lemon slice

37

HARVEY WALLBANGER

INGREDIENTS

1 × 6 out vodka, ½ × 6 out Galliano,
2 × 4 fluid ounce bottles orange juice,
5 ice cubes (shaker), 2 ice cubes (glass),
1 orange slice, straw and stirrer

PREPARATION

Place ice cubes in shaker
Add vodka and orange juice
Shake well and strain into highball glass
Add 2 ice cubes. Float Galliano on top
Garnish with slice of orange, straw and stirrer

HORSE'S NECK

INGREDIENTS

1 × 6 out brandy,
4 fluid ounces ginger ale,
1 lemon spiral,
2 ice cubes

PREPARATION

Place ice cubes in highball glass
Add brandy and spiral of lemon peel
Top with ginger ale

INSPIRATION

INGREDIENTS

2 × 6 out vodka,
½ × 6 out Benedictine,
½ × 6 out dry vermouth,
1 lemon slice,
1 cocktail cherry, 5 ice cubes

PREPARATION

Place ice cubes in bar glass

Add Benedictine, dry vermouth and vodka

Stir well and strain

Pour into chilled Paris goblet
or champagne saucer

Garnish with lemon slice and cherry on stick

JOHN COLLINS

INGREDIENTS

3 × 6 out gin, 1 × 6 out lemon juice,
1 teaspoon gomme (sugar syrup),
6 fluid ounces soda, 1 lemon slice,
1 sprig of mint, 6 ice cubes

PREPARATION

Place ice cubes in shaker. Pour in sugar syrup

Add lemon juice and gin

Shake well. Pour into chilled highball glass

Top up with soda. Stir gently

Garnish with mint and lemon slice

*Named after John Collins, head waiter at Limmers, London.
John Collins (Dry gin), Tom Collins (Old Tom Gin)*

Kir Royale

INGREDIENTS

Chilled sparkling wine (eg champagne),
2 dashes crème de cassis

PREPARATION

Place crème de cassis in well chilled
champagne saucer
Top up with chilled sparkling wine

*Canon Kir, when Parish Priest at Nolay,
decided to add crème de cassis to white Burgundy.
Today champagne, sparkling wine or
sparkling white Burgundy is used.*

*L*ASSI

INGREDIENTS

4 fluid ounces plain yoghurt,
1 tablespoon double cream,
2 tablespoon caster sugar,
1 teaspoon rose water,
ice cubes

PREPARATION

Fill shaker ½ full of ice cubes

Add all ingredients

Shake well

Pour into chilled Martini or cocktail glass

*M*ANHATTAN

INGREDIENTS

1½ × 6 out whisky, ½ × 6 out sweet vermouth,
5 ice cubes, 1 cocktail cherry, 1 cocktail stick

PREPARATION

Place ice cubes in bar glass

Add sweet vermouth and whisky

Stir well and strain. Pour into chilled lowball glass

Add cocktail cherry on stick

Originally invented in Maryland using
sugar syrup instead of vermouth to revive
a duellist in 1846, New York. In the 1890s
sweet vermouth replaced the sugar syrup and
the drink was named after the locality.

MARGARITA

INGREDIENTS

1 × 6 out Tequila, ½ × 6 out Cointreau,
½ × 6 out fresh lime juice,
ice cubes, lemon juice, salt

PREPARATION

Dip the Martini glass rim in lemon juice and redip in salt
½ fill shaker with ice cubes
Add all ingredients. Shake well
Strain into ready prepared Martini glass

Invented by a Mexican bartender in
Virginia City, USA. Named after his girlfriend,
who was accidentally shot in a street
shooting and died in his arms.

45

*M*ARTINI (DRY)

INGREDIENTS

1½ × 6 out gin,
½ × 6 out dry vermouth,
4 ice cubes, 1 olive, 1 cocktail stick

PREPARATION

Place ice cubes in bar glass
Add gin and dry vermouth
Stir well. Strain into Martini glass
Garnish with olive on stick

*Named after the bartender at the
Knickerbocker Hotel, New York 1910 –
the King of Cocktails – most
international of all cocktails*

MARTINI (MEDIUM)

INGREDIENTS

⅓ × 3 out gin,
⅓ × 3 out dry vermouth,
⅓ × 3 out sweet vermouth,
8 ice cubes

PREPARATION

Place ice cubes in bar glass
Add gin and dry and sweet vermouths
Stir well and strain
Serve in chilled Martini glass
No garnish

MARTINI (SWEET)

INGREDIENTS

1 × 6 out gin,
1 × 6 out sweet vermouth,
8 ice cubes,
1 cocktail cherry,
1 cocktail stick

PREPARATION

Place ice cubes in bar glass

Add gin and sweet vermouth

Stir well and strain

Serve in chilled Martini glass

Garnish with cocktail cherry on stick

MOSCOW MULE

INGREDIENTS

1½ × 6 out vodka, 8 fl oz ginger beer,
½ × 6 out lemon juice,
5–6 ice cubes, 1 lemon slice, 1 cucumber slice

PREPARATION

Place ice cubes in shaker

Add vodka and lemon juice. Shake well and strain

Pour into chilled highball glass

Add slices of lemon and cucumber

Top up with ginger beer. Stir and serve

*Named after Smirnoff's factory in Moscow and
produced in Los Angeles in 1947 by John Martin.
Served in a special copper mug as a gimmick*

OLD FASHIONED

INGREDIENTS

1 × 6 out rye whisky,
2 drops Angostura bitters,
1 × sugar cube,
2 × ice cubes,
1 × slice of orange

PREPARATION

Place sugar cube into lowball glass

Add Angostura bitters to sugar

Crush sugar cube

Add ice cubes, then orange slice and whisky

Stir

$\mathscr{O}$RANGE $\mathscr{B}$LOSSOM

INGREDIENTS

1 × 3 out gin,
1 × 3 out orange juice,
2 dashes Angostura bitters,
1 sprig of mint, crushed ice,
orange twist, 1 slice cucumber

PREPARATION

Fill shaker ¾ full with crushed ice

Add Angostura bitters, gin and orange juice

Shake and strain

Pour into chilled cocktail glass

Garnish with sprig of mint if available

or orange twist and cucumber

PARSON'S SPECIAL

INGREDIENTS

4 fluid ounces orange juice,
1 egg yolk,
2 teaspoon grenadine,
soda water, ice cubes,
1 slice kiwi fruit, 1 strawberry

PREPARATION

Fill shaker ¾ full with ice cubes

Add all ingredients

Shake well

Strain into old fashioned glass

Top up with soda water

Stir and garnish with kiwi fruit and strawberry

PIMMS No 1

INGREDIENTS

1 × 3 out Pimms,
6 fluid ounces lemonade, 4 ice cubes,
Fruit: orange slices, lemon slices, cucumber slices,
cucumber peel, apple slices, 1 strawberry,
sprig mint, bee-borage, 2 straws

PREPARATION

Place Pimms in highball or Pimms glass.

Add ice cubes and fruit. Top up with lemonade.

Garnish with fruit, mint and bee-borage

Serve with straws

*The recipe for the world's first Gin Sling was invented
by James Pimms of Pimms' Oyster Bar, a stone's throw
from the City of London. The world famous Pimms No 1
cup today is based on fine gin and other secret ingredients.*

PINACOLADA

INGREDIENTS

1 × 6 out rum,
1 × 3 out coconut cream,
4 fluid ounces pineapple juice,
10 ice cubes, 1 cocktail stick,
1 pineapple chunk,
slither of fresh coconut

PREPARATION

Place ice in shaker

Add rum, coconut cream and pineapple juice

Shake well and strain

Serve in chilled highball glass

Garnish with coconut and pineapple on stick

*P*INK *G*IN

INGREDIENTS

1 × 6 out gin,
1 dash Angostura bitters,
2 × 6 out iced water

PREPARATION

Place Angostura bitters in Paris goblet
and swill around glass
Add gin
Top up with iced water

Associated with the officers of the Royal Navy.
Was probably invented in the West Indies

PINK LADY

INGREDIENTS

1 × 6 out gin,
1 × 6 out calvados,
1 × 6 out lime juice,
5 dashes grenadine,
crushed ice, 1 slice of lime,
1 cocktail cherry, 1 cocktail stick

PREPARATION

Fill shaker ½ full with crushed ice

Add gin, calvados, lime juice and grenadine

Shake well and strain

Pour into sugar frosted cocktail glass

Garnish with lime and cocktail cherry on stick

*P*LANTER'S *P*UNCH

INGREDIENTS

1 × 6 out rum, 2 fluid ounces orange juice,
2 fluid ounces pineapple juice,
2 barspoons grenadine, 10 ice cubes,
1 cocktail stick, 1 orange slice, 1 pineapple chunk

PREPARATION

Place ice in shaker

Add rum and orange juice, pineapple juice and grenadine

Shake well and strain

Serve in chilled highball glass

Garnish with orange slice and pineapple chunk on stick

PRAIRIE OYSTER

INGREDIENTS

1 egg yolk, 1 dash Cayenne pepper,
1 teaspoon Worcester sauce,
1 teaspoon tomato ketchup,
2 dashes vinegar

PREPARATION

Place all ingredients in Paris goblet and stir
To be drunk in one gulp!

*A drink given to a sick invalid who requested
oysters but was given egg yolks instead! He recovered!*

𝒫USSY ℱOOT

INGREDIENTS

1 × 3 out orange juice,
1 × 3 out lemon juice,
1 × 3 out lime juice,
1 × 6 out grenadine,
1 egg yolk, crushed ice,
soda, 1 strawberry, 2 straws

PREPARATION

Fill shaker ¾ full with crushed ice

Add fruit juices, grenadine and egg yolk

Shake well and strain

Pour into highball glass. Top up with soda

Garnish with strawberry and straws

RAISIN & GINGER PUNCH

INGREDIENTS

4 fluid ounces apple juice, 4 fluid ounces ginger ale,
1 × 6 out lemon juice, 1 teaspoon clear honey,
1 teaspoon raisins, 2 lemon zest spirals,
sprigs of mint, lemon slices, crushed ice, 2 straws

PREPARATION

Fill shaker ¼ full with crushed ice
Add lemon juice and zest, honey, raisins and apple juice
Shake well. Pour ice and mixture into Collins glass
Add ginger ale. Stir well
Garnish with lemon slices, mint and straws

ROB ROY

INGREDIENTS

1½ × 6 out whisky,
½ × 6 out sweet vermouth,
1 cocktail cherry,
1 cocktail stick,
7 ice cubes

PREPARATION

Place ice cubes in bar glass

Add whisky and sweet vermouth

Stir well and strain

Serve in chilled Martini glass

Garnish with cocktail cherry on stick

*R*UM *C*OLLINS

INGREDIENTS

1½ × 6 out rum (white), 1½ × 6 out lemon juice,
1 × 6 out gomme (sugar syrup), 1 lemon slice,
1 cocktail cherry, 1 cocktail stick, 4–5 ice cubes,
2 straws, soda

PREPARATION

Place ice cubes in shaker

Add lemon juice, sugar syrup and rum

Shake well. Do not strain

Pour into chilled Collins glass

Top up with soda and stir

Garnish with lemon slice and cocktail cherry on stick

Serve with straws

*S*T *C*LEMENT'S

INGREDIENTS

4 fluid ounces orange juice,
4 fluid ounces bitter lemon,
crushed ice, 1 lemon slice,
1 orange slice, straw

PREPARATION

Fill shaker ¼ full with crushed ice

Add orange juice

Shake well

Pour ice and orange juice into Collins glass

Add bitter lemon and stir

Decorate with lemon and orange slice

Serve with straw

SANGRIA

INGREDIENTS

5 fluid ounces red table wine,
1 × 6 out brandy, 1 × 3 out orange juice,
4 fluid ounces lemonade,
cut oranges, cut lemon,
3 ice cubes (glass), ice for bar glass

PREPARATION

Place ice cubes and cut fruit in highball glass
Place ice cubes in bar glass and add wine
Add orange juice and brandy
Add lemonade and stir to blend
Strain into chilled glass

Traditional Spanish drink

SCOTCH MIST

INGREDIENTS

2 × 6 out whisky,
1 sprig of mint,
crushed ice,
2 short straws

PREPARATION

Fill old fashioned glass ¾ full with crushed ice

Place mint leaves on ice

Pour on whisky and stir

Serve with straws

𝒮CREWDRIVER

INGREDIENTS

1 × 3 out vodka,
4 fluid ounces orange juice,
crushed ice, 1 orange slice,
1 cocktail cherry

PREPARATION

Fill shaker ¼ full with crushed ice

Add vodka and orange juice

Shake well

Strain into old fashioned glass

Garnish with orange slice and cherry on stick

*Another gimmick drink produced by John Martin using
vodka; it soon became a craze which has survived*

SHIRLEY TEMPLE

INGREDIENTS

4 fluid ounces ginger ale,
1 teaspoon grenadine,
cocktail cherries, 8 ice cubes, straws

PREPARATION

Place ice cubes into highball glass

Add ginger ale

Add grenadine

Stir slightly

Garnish with cherries and straws

*S*IDECAR

INGREDIENTS

1 × 6 out brandy, 1 × 6 out Cointreau,
1 × 6 out lemon juice, crushed ice,
1 orange slice, 1 lemon slice,
1 cocktail cherry, 1 cocktail stick

PREPARATION

Fill shaker ¾ full with crushed ice

Add brandy, Cointreau and lemon juice

Shake well and strain. Serve in chilled cocktail glass

Garnish with orange, lemon and cherry on stick

*One of classics associated with Harry's
New York Bar, Paris in 1911. Invented for a
customer who arrived at the bar in a sidecar*

𝒮TINGER

INGREDIENTS

1½ × 6 brandy,
½ × 6 white crème de menthe,
sprigs of mint, 8–9 ice cubes

PREPARATION

Place ice cubes in shaker
Add crème de menthe and brandy
Shake well and strain
Serve in chilled brandy balloon
Garnish with mint

TEA PUNCH

INGREDIENTS

2 fluid ounces cold tea,
4 fluid ounces orange juice,
1 × 6 out lemon juice, 1 × 3 out raspberry juice,
1 × 3 out pineapple juice,
soda, ice cubes,
1 orange slice, 1 lemon slice

PREPARATION

Fill shaker ½ full ice cubes

Add tea and fruit juices

Shake well. Place in highball glass

Top up with soda water

Garnish with fruit slices

TEQUILA SUNRISE

INGREDIENTS

1 × 6 out Tequila, 3 × 6 out orange juice,
2 barspoons grenadine, 10 ice cubes,
1 orange slice, 1 cocktail cherry, 1 cocktail stick

PREPARATION

Place ice cubes in shaker. Add Tequila and orange juice

Shake well. Strain mixture into chilled Martini
or highball glass and slowly pour in grenadine

Allow to settle. Garnish with orange and cherry on stick

Just before serving stir once

*Name taken from early Spanish settlement in Mexico
where a distillery to make spirit from a national brew
was established. Sunrise is the visual effect of the drink.*

WHISKY SOUR

INGREDIENTS

1 × 3 out whisky,
1 × 3 out lemon juice,
6 dashes gomme (sugar syrup),
crushed ice, 1 orange slice,
1 cocktail cherry,
1 cocktail stick

PREPARATION

Fill shaker ¾ full with crushed ice

Add whisky, lemon juice and sugar syrup

Shake well and strain

Serve in sour glass

Garnish with orange slice and cocktail cherry on stick

WHITE LADY

INGREDIENTS

1 × 6 out gin,
1 × 6 out Cointreau,
1 × 6 out lemon juice,
crushed ice, 1 lemon slice,
1 cocktail cherry, 1 cocktail stick

PREPARATION

Fill shaker ¾ full with crushed ice
Add gin, Cointreau and lemon juice
Shake well and strain
Serve in chilled cocktail glass
Garnish with lemon slice and cherry on stick

Another creation from Harry's New York Bar, Paris

YELLOW DWARF

INGREDIENTS

1 egg yolk,
1 × 3 out cream,
1 × 3 out orgeat syrup,
maraschino cherry, ice cubes,
soda

PREPARATION

Fill shaker ½ full with ice cubes

Add egg yolk, cream and orgeat syrup

Shake well

Strain into cocktail glass

Top up with soda

Garnish with cherry

*Z*OMBIE *V*OODOO

INGREDIENTS

1 × 6 out rum (golden), 1 × 6 out rum (white),
½ × 6 out rum (dark), 1 × 6 out lime juice,
1 × 6 out orange juice, 3 drops Angostura bitters,
½ × 6 out gomme (sugar syrup), 1 egg white, ice cubes,
2 straws, 1 orange slice, 1 lemon slice, 1 pineapple chunk,
1 cocktail cherry, 1 cocktail stick, 1 sprig of mint

PREPARATION

Fill shaker ½ full with ice cubes
Add rums, juices, sugar syrup, egg white and Angostura bitters
Shake well. Do not strain
Pour into Collins glass
Garnish with fruit slices, pineapple, cherry and mint

COLOUR-CODED INDEX

RUM

Bacardi 9
Cuba Libre 24
Daiquiri 26
Pinacolada 54
Planter's Punch 57
Rum Collins 62
Zombie Voodoo 75

VODKA

Black Russian 12
Bloody Mary 14
Cavendish 20
Forester 31
Harvey Wallbanger 38
Inspiration 40
Moscow Mule 49
Screwdriver 66

WINE

American Glory 6
Black Velvet 13
Bucks Fizz 19
Champagne
    Cocktail 21
Kir Royale 42
Sangria 64

OTHERS

Americano 5
Appleknocker 7
Egg Nogg 29
Fernet Branca 30
Margarita 45
Pimms No 1 53
Tequila Sunrise 71

ACKNOWLEDGEMENTS

The author and publishers would like to thank the following for their help in the preparation of this book.

Photographs: Eric Pelham, 79 Wilding Road, Wallingford, Oxon (Tel: 0491 33568)
Photographic assistance: Philip Millington-Hawes
Cocktail preparation: Andrew Durkan
Glasses: loaned by Bentalls plc, 1 Ealing Broadway Centre, Ealing, London W5 and Ealing College of Higher Education
Bar facilities: Ealing College of Higher Education

All the cocktails illustrated in this book were prepared using the correct ingredients.

The publishers would also like to thank the Mary Evans Picture Library for permission to use the photographs on pages vii, viii, xvi, xvii and xviii.